JOY

ALSO BY KATHI PELTON
Peace (formerly *Stepping into Peace*)
Courage (formerly *Becoming Bold and Courageous*)
Finding Home: A Doorway of Hope

(with Jeffrey Pelton)
The Yielding: A Lifestyle of Surrender
The Songs of Christmas

CONTRIBUTOR
Prophet Sharing 2021
Prophet Sharing 2022

JOY

Kathi Pelton

Inscribe Press
Creativity Unleashed

Copyright ©2022 Kathi Pelton. All rights reserved.
For permission to use or reproduce portions of this work (other than brief quotations for reviews) please write to: admin@inscribepress.com.

Published by Inscribe Press, Hillsboro, OR
Cover design by Kathi Pelton and Amy Tanner

Printed in the United States of America

ISBN (paperback) 978-1-951611-47-7
  (eBook) 978-1-951611-49-1

Unless otherwise noted, Scripture quotations are taken from the Holy Bible, New Living Translation, copyright © 1996, 2004, 2015 by Tyndale House Foundation. Used by permission of Tyndale House Publishers, Carol Stream, Illinois 60188, USA. All rights reserved.

Scripture quotations marked CJB taken from the Complete Jewish Bible by David H. Stern. Copyright © 1998. All rights reserved. Used by permission of Messianic Jewish Publishers, 6120 Day Long Lane, Clarksville, MD 21029. www.messianicjewish.net.

Scripture quotations marked KJV taken from the King James Bible.

Contents

Foreword by Anita Alexander vii
Preface by Jeffrey Pelton xi
ONE An Introduction to True Joy 1
TWO Forming a Mindset of Joy 5
THREE The Plumb Line that Brings Joy 9
FOUR Hope Brings Joy 13
FIVE Joy Comes in the Morning 17
SIX Let Peace and Joy Kiss 21
SEVEN Fruitful in Joy 25
EIGHT Enter into Joy 29
NINE Joy in Righteousness 35
TEN Restoring Joy 39
ELEVEN The Fear of the LORD Makes Room for Joy 43
TWELVE Joy in Stillness 47
THIRTEEN The Joyful Dance 51
FOURTEEN The Blood Brings Joy 55
FIFTEEN Fellowship with Joy 59
SIXTEEN Joy is Healing 63
SEVENTEEN Comfort and Joy 69
EIGHTEEN Joy in the Little Things 73

TWENTY Joy Washes over Me 81
TWENTY-ONE Joyful Expectation 85
TWENTY-TWO Joy is a Key 91
TWENTY-THREE The Still Waters of Joy 95
TWENTY-FOUR Overwhelming Joy 99
TWENTY-FIVE Grace is Spelled J-O-Y 103
TWENTY-SIX The Joy of Being Known 107
TWENTY-SEVEN Healing Joy 111
TWENTY-EIGHT The Joy of New Beginnings 115
TWENTY-NINE Joyful Trust 121
THIRTY Joy's Embrace 125
About the Author 129

Foreword

Kathi's devotional on joy couldn't come at a more crucial time in the seasons we as a body of Christ are navigating in this hour. Joy is truly one of the unsung heroes of our inheritance in Christ. One of my favourite scriptures on joy is in Nehemiah 8:10, "The joy of the Lord is your strength." In the Hebrew it means that the joy of the Lord provides a fortified place of protection. As we stand in an hour where there has been a significant acceleration of the forces of darkness waging war against the sons of light, strength and protection found in kingdom joy is surely part of the battle strategy in securing victory on all sides.

Romans 14:17 explains that the kingdom of God is neither food nor drink but righteousness, peace, and joy in the Holy Spirit. That means joy is one third of the kingdom of God! In Matthew 6:33, Jesus summoned us to pursue the kingdom of God first; in other words make it a priority above all else, and all the things the heathen seek will be added to us. Wow, what an exhortation! Unfortunately, many times we can find ourselves seeking other things first, believing whether consciously or subconsciously that joy will come as a result in us obtaining that which we seek. We seek to fortify and protect ourselves with accomplishments and achievements in this natural realm, only to find that when trouble or unforeseen circumstances occur, our house of joy we have built in our own strength comes crashing down (Matthew 7:24-27). It may not be material possessions—it could be success in our achievements, a spouse, a career, a ministry, a reputation, even justice in a situation. Regardless of what it is, if our pursuit in obtaining those things is rooted in the belief that it is our source of joy then we aren't positioned in seeking first the kingdom and the kingdom kind of joy is a joy that isn't measured by natural circumstance. Kingdom joy flows from the Holy Spirit as Romans 14:17 explains.

Our saviour beautifully explains in John 15 how this kingdom kind of joy is discovered. He teaches us what it looks like to abide in him. Doing relationship with Jesus is like no other. As we respond to the invitation of the vinedresser of our life, we embark on a journey of sweet surrender that unlocks the kingdom of God that is within (Luke 17:21). In verse 11 of John 15, Jesus drops the bomb of how doing relationship with him causes the well of kingdom joy to overflow in our life.

> "I have told you these things, that My joy and delight may be in you, and that your joy and gladness may be of full measure and complete and overflowing."

Wow! Joy that is complete and full in our lives comes from abiding in him and obeying his commandments! It's a pursuit of intimacy with our saviour and yielding to his gracious hand that tends to the vine of our hearts.

Truly if joy is something that has evaded your life in these past seasons or in your life in general, this devotional is heaven's kiss to you. As you read through the daily encouragements followed by devotional scriptures to meditate upon and pray through, you will begin to experience that longed-for heart transformation take place. By delving into the pages of this book you have set your heart to pursue first the kingdom of God. You have made the decision to allow the word of God that is so beautifully unpacked by Kathi in the pages of this book, to invade your yearning heart.

As Kathi's signature mother's heart invades the pages of this book, your heart will encounter a healing and resurrection life-giving anointing. The well of her history with God shared in her personal testimonies and encounters with him aid and invite the reader into operating in a kingdom way that has the power to break you loose from cycles of despair, depression, fear, and worry, and will renew and revive your trust in God, truly restoring you back to the "JOY" of your salvation (Psalm 51:12).

I'm excited for you, friend. Take hold of this gift from God ministered through the Kathi's writings. This is your divine appointment, the one you have been praying for. You truly will find a joy unspeakable and full of glory (1 Peter 1:8).

Blessings.

ANITA ALEXANDER
Prophetic Revivalist, Author, Co-Senior Minister
Golden City Church, Gold Coast, Queensland, Australia

Preface

This is the third book in a series originally titled *30 Days to Breakthrough*. In 2021, when Kathi started writing about joy (despite walking through one of the most difficult times in her life; you can read about it in chapter seventeen), we decided it was time to reformat the series, so this and the previous two books would have a fresher look.

The content of the previous books has not changed, so if you have one or both of the previous editions, don't run out and buy the new ones—unless, of course, you want them.

Why are these books arranged in short chapters covering thirty days? Is there something special about that length of time? Is there an obscure biblical mandate that we have unearthed in one of the prophetic books of Scripture? Or is this some sort of spacey, New Age thinking?

The short answer is that God originally spoke to Kathi several years ago about stepping into a new lifestyle of peace by spending thirty days allowing him to change her thinking, taking her into a new realm of trust in him. This resulted in the first book, *Stepping into Peace*.

The concept of taking thirty days to develop a new mindset is consistent with many psychological studies about human behavior. Change takes intentionality and effort, and setting aside a specified period for readjustment is extremely helpful. Thirty days may not magically catapult you into a new lifestyle, but it is definitely long enough to get a good jump start.

That is the reason for what you are about to read. The more we allow the Holy Spirit to impart his character and fruit in us, the greater our trust grows in his goodness and we find ourselves responding to him and following his counsel, rather than reacting to circumstances and trouble around us. This book, like the two before it, are meant to aid the bride of Christ in her quest to discover and experience more of the love and faithfulness of her beloved Bridegroom, and find comfort by trusting more deeply in his care.

One of the values of Christian teaching and literature is that we are afforded the opportunity to discover how others have walked the roads we all must travel. It is a little like reading someone's diary.

You will read about failures and triumphs, sorrows and joys, and the richness of life lived as part of the magnificent domain we call the kingdom of God.

JEFFREY PELTON

DAY ONE
An Introduction to True Joy

Joy—true biblical joy—is not merely a momentary reaction to good news, a day of celebration, or a happy event. True joy is found in the confident assurance and hope that the eternal promise we have been given through Christ Jesus and his Word will surely come to pass.

When Jesus endured the cross, the Bible says,

> ...Because of the joy awaiting him, he endured the cross, disregarding its shame. Now He is seated in the place of honor beside God's throne.
> (Hebrews 12:2)

How can there be joy mentioned in such a passage? The joy spoken of in Hebrews 12 is what Jesus focused on as he went through the most agonizing time any person has ever faced. For he not only took upon the physical brutality of the scourging and the crucifixion, but he took upon himself the weight and penalty of the sin of all mankind. He paid the price that we could not pay and could not have endured. Yet, he understood the true joy set before him that would make the price worth the prize.

As we have entered a time throughout the earth where fear, anxiety and weeping have come upon mankind in a way that no one anticipated; it is vital that we, too, understand the joy set before us. Though darkness has descended upon the earth and upon mankind, there is an eternal hope for a Kingdom "yet to come" who's author and finisher is the Lord. The light of his love and his promise of a future and a hope that prospers us is illuminated in a far greater way amid darkness. The joy of what is set before us helps us to endure the times of weeping, for we know that the morning will come!

> For his anger lasts but a moment but his favor lasts a lifetime! Weeping may last through the night, but joy comes in the morning. (Psalm 30:5)

The next thirty days we will explore what joy truly is, and we will reach for that joy so that it is continually set before us as our hope and our confident assurance of his faithfulness. He is our good news, our reason to celebrate, and our happy event as we wake up every morning knowing that nothing can separate us from his love. Today is the first day of opening a doorway to joy. Your focus will be reset from the narrative of the world and the destruction that resounds in its airwaves, to the truth that there is an unspeakable joy to be discovered and enjoyed in Jesus.

Day One Verse

Without having seen him, you love him. Without seeing him now, but trusting in him, you continue to be full of joy that is glorious beyond words. And you are receiving what your trust is aiming at, namely, your deliverance.
(1 Peter 1:8-9, CJB)

DAY ONE PRAYER

Holy Spirit, I eagerly desire to discover and apprehend true and lasting joy. Jesus, I long to experience "the joy that was set before you" when you endured the cross; for that is a joy that is not conditional upon circumstances or the world around me. I yield my life to you and ask for a revelation of the unspeakable joy that delivers me from all oppression and worry. I want to aim my trust at what is set before me. Help me throughout these next thirty days to reset my heart and mind on the joy of knowing you. Come, Holy Spirit, and help me to move into a joy that cannot be stolen from me and gives me an endurance that does not leave me lacking. Amen.

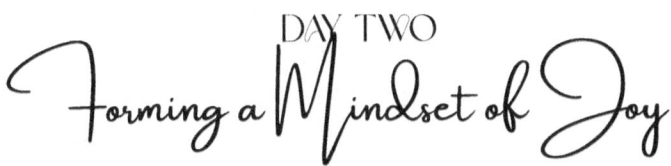
Day Two
Forming a Mindset of Joy

As a man thinketh in his heart, so is he.
(Proverbs 23:7, KJV)

Now, that is a verse to chew on for a while! A phrase that I often hear used in the church is, "Get rid of stinking thinking." There are a lot of thoughts in our hearts that need to be changed and purified. Somehow many believers walk in the conviction of being sure that they speak lovingly and have edifying thoughts about their neighbor, but they give themselves free permission to speak harshly and think negative thoughts about themselves. It is not humility to be self-deprecating; it is sin. Yet, it exists within the church as much as we see it outside the church (maybe more).

This "stinking thinking" regarding ourselves is one of the biggest joy killers there is. How do you have joy when you hate yourself? Matthew 22:37-40 says,

> Jesus replied: "Love the Lord your God with all your heart and with all your soul and with all your

mind." This is the first and greatest commandment. And the second is like it: "Love your neighbor as yourself." All the Law and the Prophets hang on these two commandments.

What if the reason that the church is having a hard time loving their neighbor is that they have not learned to love themselves? The truth is that most people do love themselves enough to take care of their health, their personal needs, and even to pursue their desires, but their thoughts about themselves can be harsh, cynical, and condemning. A condemned man cannot experience joy!

I believe that the Lord would have every believer align their self-thoughts with his thoughts toward them. If your thoughts toward yourself have been negative and harsh, then today is a good day to change that. They say it takes at least thirty days to change a habit, so you are already a day behind! Ask the Lord to forgive you for the harsh judgements that you have had against yourself, and then ask the Holy Spirit to come and reveal God's thoughts toward you. The Word of God is filled with passages about God's thoughts toward his children. Here is just one.

> Your eyes saw my substance, being yet unformed. And in Your book they all were written, the days fashioned for me, when as yet there were none of them. How precious also are Your thoughts to me, O God! How great is the sum of them!
> (Psalm 139:16-17)

How great is the sum of his thoughts toward you! Now, that is a reason for true joy. These are good thoughts, prospering thoughts, loving thoughts, and thoughts that transform us into all he created us for. Honestly, we could spend thirty days on this subject alone because if we are what we believe in our hearts, then we need a heart change.

Day Two Verse

I delight greatly in the LORD;
my soul rejoices in my God.
For he has clothed me with garments of salvation
and arrayed me in a robe of his righteousness,
as a bridegroom adorns his head like a priest,
and as a bride adorns herself with her jewels.
(Isaiah 61:10)

DAY TWO PRAYER

Lord, I want to think about myself the way that you think about me. Your Word says that "as a man thinketh in his heart, so is he." Therefore, I want to think your thoughts and have them planted in my heart as my truth and my reality. Forgive me for giving myself permission to be harsh with "me." Spirit of God, come and purify my heart from every negative belief that exists in my heart and comes forth from my mouth as curses against my identity and character. I repent and turn from harsh judgements again myself. Create in me a pure heart regarding *me*! Renew a right spirit within me so that I can think in a way that is becoming of who you made me and then become that man (woman). Thank you for revealing this to me and for changing my heart and my thoughts so that I can live in joy.

DAY THREE

The Plumb Line that Brings Joy

One day, as I was praying for a couple that was in a difficult place in their lives and experiencing an extreme wrestle with disappointment and hopelessness, I was taken into a vision for them where a plumb line came down from heaven and was hanging over their lives. The disappointments and hopelessness were causing their heads to hang down, causing them only to see the wind and the waves. But the Lord spoke and said, "Tell them to look up and surrender their lives to the plumb line of the Lord, so that will cause all things to come into alignment with My plans, purposes, and steps."

There is a yielding and surrender that we are invited to enter that says to the Lord, "Not my will, but your will be done." There are times and seasons where the enemy comes to kill, steal, and destroy the plans and purposes in our lives that were set there to bring glory to his name. It is in those times that we are not to succumb to the warfare, but we are to rise up and ask for the plumb line of the Lord to align us once again with the abundant life that he has promised us.

> "The thief comes only to steal and kill and destroy;
> I came that they may have life and have it in abundance." (John 10:10)

The "thief" that Jesus spoke of is normally thought of as the enemy (Satan), and though he is a true thief who seeks to kill and destroy, Jesus is also speaking of failed leadership (if you put the verse in the context of the whole chapter). Often the failure of godly governments, earthly systems, and leaders with selfish motives ruled by demonic agendas releases on people injustice of destruction and death. God is offering us a way out from under the rule of ungodly government and leadership into a divine and righteous government that is upon his shoulders. Though we live on earth, we can have lives ruled by heaven's perfect order that brings us into a place of victory, overcoming, and abundance. Within the mercy and justice of his leadership and dominion over our lives, we receive great joy. No longer are we under the weight and burden of failed leadership, but we have yielded our lives to the perfect leader, the King of Kings, who reigns in justice and mercy.

The enemy wants us to believe that we are trapped and caught in his web of oppression that comes from a place of failed and flawed leadership, when all along, we have been invited into the abundant life that comes when we live in the sovereignty of his government and his Kingdom. When we begin to lose sight of that truth, we need to ask for his plumb line to realign us with truth and with his justice and mercy. As we do this, it is like coming under the direct flow of favor and blessings that come from the Father of Lights.

> Every good gift and every perfect gift is from above, and cometh down from the Father of lights, with whom is no variableness, neither shadow of turning.
> (James 1:17)
>
> This then is the message which we have heard of him, and declare unto you, that God is light, and in him is no darkness at all. (1 John 1:5)

We can live in the darkness of despair, or the joy of His glorious light. As we remain in him, there is only light that brings great joy. There may be darkness all around, but we are found in the light and receive the blessings and gifts that come from the Father of Light. It is our choice. We can choose to remain under the tyranny of failed leadership that leads us into darkness and despair, or we can live under the rule and dominion of the King of Heaven, where there is only light that brings great joy. There is no shadow of turning in him. If shadows begin to appear, it may be that you have veered or turned and need to come back under the plumb line that brings light.

Day Three Verse

But let all who take refuge in you rejoice;
let them sing joyful praises forever.
Spread your protection over them,
that all who love your name may be filled with joy.
For you bless the godly, O LORD;
you surround them with your shield of love.
(Psalm 5:11-12)

DAY THREE PRAYER:

Father, right now, I invite your heavenly plumb line to be held over my life. The darkness and shadows have been filtering your light and causing me to see dimly. The thief seeks to rob joy from me and keep me from the glorious abundant life that you came to give. Forgive me for losing sight of your light and for giving into the darkness of despair. I now yield and surrender every aspect of my life to the perfect alignment with your plans, steps, and purposes for my life. Holy Spirit, align every part so that I can experience the joy of living in the light of your love and your favor. I declare you as my King, the perfect leader of my life. I submit to your authority and rule in my life and my heart. Thank you that you are the only perfect shepherd, leader, and Father over my life.

DAY FOUR
Hope Brings Joy

The life of a believer is filled with mountains and valleys, yet the one thing that should not waver in either place is hope. To lose hope is to abandon faith, and to abandon faith is to deny God.

The Book of Job says this,

> You will be secure, because there is hope, and you will look around and lie down in safety. You will lie down without fear, and many will court your favor. But the eyes of the wicked will fail, and escape will elude them; they will hope for their last breath.
> (Job 11:18-20)

To lose faith leaves men only hoping for their last breath. Hope is what gives our faith confidence, and confidence is what gives us joy in hope; because the love of God never disappoints.

In my twenties, I went through many years of infertility. My husband and I longed for a baby, but month after month, year after year—no baby came. Yet, through the pain, there was hope that brought joy to the dreams of one day having a family together. Had hope merely left us in despair, it would not have been rooted in our faith in God. Faith, hope, and joy are eternally connected. If you have faith, then you have hope, and if you have hope, then there is a reason for joy! The presence of joy does not assure the absence of pain because I am talking about an unwavering joy that is based in your faith and hope in Jesus Christ.

The joy that I maintained through those difficult years was not based on whether I would conceive a child (which I did after adopting a baby girl), but it was based on the love of God that was poured out upon me day by day. There was pain in the longing but joy in the love that was poured out to comfort my pain. This joy cannot be described as "happiness," but rather as deep confidence and contentment in the state of being deeply loved.

> And hope does not put us to shame, because God's love has been poured out into our hearts through the Holy Spirit, who has been given to us.
> (Romans 5:5)

How can we be put to shame when the love of God has been poured out in us, and his Spirit has been given to us? We are highly favored and deeply honored by the God of all creation. Though we may finish our race here on earth without every desire fulfilled or every prayer answered, we are not without hope, and we are not without joy! His faithful love will never leave or forsake us, and we will forever be surrounded by the goodness of God as displayed in his unfailing love.

Day Four Verse

You make known to me the path of life; in your presence there is fullness of joy; at your right hand are pleasures forevermore. (Psalm 16:11)

Day Four Prayer

Thank you, Jesus, that I am not without hope and that the hope in your eternal promise brings me great joy. I ask Lord that you would cause to be my strength and my song. Wash away the areas that despair and hopelessness have crept into my soul as I lost sight of your unfailing love that is poured into my life daily. I let go of mindset that says that the only way to have joy is to be happy in circumstantial and momentary fulfillment. I desire my joy to be the unshakeable, immoveable, and unsearchable love of God. Thank you for giving me your Spirit and for pouring out your love in my heart.

DAY FIVE
Joy Comes in the Morning

After the miraculous adoption of our oldest daughter and the equally miraculous birth of our oldest son, God granted us another pregnancy. My husband and I were overjoyed that we did not face years of infertility and the treatments for infertility once again. We spent our Thanksgiving and Christmas season with great excitement as we fell in love with the little one growing in my womb. There had been such a difficult struggle adopting our daughter (even losing her once) and getting pregnant with our son, but this baby came unexpectantly and with such joy.

When I was five months pregnant, I woke up one morning hemorrhaging. Fear, unbelief, and shock gripped us as we drove to the doctor's office. After unsuccessfully trying to find our little one's heartbeat and an examination that confirmed that our baby had died in my womb, we were sent to the hospital to have our precious baby taken from inside of me. The pain was unimaginable, and the loss was keenly felt even before the surgeons took her from me; yes, it was a baby girl.

When I woke up from the surgery, the grief flooded me like someone who had her most precious possession robbed straight from her arms. I did not get to hold her or to say goodbye. Jeff and I felt so empty.

When we arrived home, we were surrounded by friends and family that came to hold us, weep with us, and take care of our young children while we grieved. Amid the ache, the Lord was so very present. It would have been unbearable if he had not been with us to comfort us and remind us that our little girl, Alexandra Hope, was safe in his arms.

It took time to heal, to "feel" hope again, and to dream again. But, once again, there was joy amid the grief because the greatness of his love was so near to us. No one could rob us of his love or of knowing that our daughter was experiencing the eternal joy that we all hope and long for. She would never experience sin, pain, or disappointment. She went from my womb to the womb of all creation.

Two years later, we were once again in the hospital, but this time, a baby girl was being placed in our arms—a healthy, beautiful baby girl. God had restored what had been taken. We named her Amy, which means "Beloved." There are times of deep grief and tragedies that cause us to gasp in shock, but our God is a god of restoration, comfort, healing, and faithfulness. We continually live as prisoners of hope for the eternal joy that is just ahead for those who love him and have been called according to his purposes. You are his beloved one.

Day Five Verse

Sing praises to the LORD, O you his saints, and give thanks to his holy name. For his anger is but for a moment, and his favor is for a lifetime. Weeping may tarry for the night, but joy comes with the morning.
(Psalm 30:4-5)

DAY FIVE PRAYER

God, this world is not without loss or grief, but You are our comfort during all our pain and sorrows. Though we all face seasons of sorrow, we know that "weeping may last for the night, but joy comes with the morning." Surely, morning comes, and we experience the joy that is always before us. I pray that you would heal my soul from the traumas that I have experienced in my life and comfort me in the losses that have touched my days. I choose to find my joy in that which can never be taken away; your love, your presence, and your faithfulness to restore my life. I give thanks to you and sing praises for your favor!

DAY SIX

> And the peace of God, which transcends all understanding, will guard your hearts and mind in Christ Jesus. (Philippians 4:7)

Most of my morning prayers begin with asking for the peace of God to guard my heart and my mind throughout the day ahead. I have learned that when God's peace, which transcends our understanding or circumstances, is established in our lives, joy quickly takes its hand.

Peace and joy are like an inseparable couple that has kissed the lives of the believer. It is difficult to have one without the other. In my first book in this series, originally titled *Stepping Into Peace*, I tell a story of how God began my personal journey to establish peace. It is worth repeating.

Many years ago, I had the Lord ask me a question that caught me by surprise. He asked me, "What is the greatest cause of warfare in your life?"

I knew not to answer quickly because the Lord rarely asks me questions, but when he does, it is rarely the obvious answer. After many hours of thought, I finally decided to answer his question with a question. "Lord, what is the greatest source of warfare in my life?" Once again, his answer surprised me.

"Daughter, it is your lack of peace. If you had my peace that surpasses understanding, then you would not be experiencing so much warfare in your soul."

From that day on, the Lord began taking me on a journey to establish peace in my life. As his peace was being established in more and more areas in my life, I was beginning to experience a joy that I had not known before. It was beyond just a feeling of happiness—it was a deep foundational joy that came from the presence of peace in my life. Peace washed away the stress, worry, and constant anxiety that had plagued my life. It ushered in a new trust, confidence, and rest that made room for true joy. The presence of peace is the absence of chaos, and the presence of joy causes the sorrows of yesterday to fade away.

> "Peace I leave with you; my peace I give you. I do not give to you as the world gives. Do not let your hearts be troubled and do not be afraid."
> (John 14:27)

The Hebrew word for peace is *shalom*, which is mentioned over 420 times in the Bible. The meaning of peace, or *shalom*, is completeness, wholeness, health, welfare, safety, soundness, tranquility, prosperity, fullness, rest, harmony, the absence of agitation or discord, and a state of calm without anxiety or stress. What a great gift is wrapped up in the package called "peace"! No wonder joy accompanies it.

No longer must we live with troubled hearts, because God has left us his peace and filled us with his Spirit, who gives us everlasting peace.

Day Six Verse

May the God of hope fill you with all joy and peace in believing, so that by the power of the Holy Spirit you may abound in hope. (Romans 15:13)

Day Six Prayer

God, I am tired of endless warfare, worry, and anxiety. I need the peace (the *shalom*) that only you can give. This world has established a constant war within my soul that steals joy, steals peace, and steals my trust in you. I surrender and yield my body, soul, and spirit to your Spirit, which brings everlasting peace, joy, and hope. I invite you to take me on the journey to see peace established in my soul. I want peace to guard my heart and mind. I lay down every anxious thought that leads me to fear and dread, and I receive your peace that brings me joy and hope. Restore my soul! I need your still waters and green pastures of refreshing. Fill me, even this day, with joy and peace so that I may abound in hope!

DAY SEVEN
Fruitful in Joy

Have you ever noticed that if you put a rotten piece of fruit in a bowl full of good fruit, the whole bowl will go bad? That is where the saying, "One bad apple can spoil the whole bunch?" comes from. This is because a piece of rotten fruit releases a gas called ethylene, which causes all the fruit in a bowl to ripen quickly, leading them to rot.

Joy is a fruit of the Spirit, but when you put it in the bowl of your life along with some rotten fruit, it will spoil the fruit of joy. The tolerated, or allowed, existence of rage, harsh judgements, pride, malice, slander, bitterness, and things such as this is what I would call rotten fruit. They let off a spiritual gas that ruins the good fruit.

> Finally, brothers, whatever is true, whatever is honorable, whatever is just, whatever is pure, whatever is lovely, whatever is commendable, if there is any excellence, if there is anything worthy of praise, think about these things. (Philippians 4:8)

When I was a new believer, I sure had a lot of rotten fruit in the bowl of my life. I had spent many years filling my mind with counterfeit beliefs and ungodly thoughts. Manipulating to gain what I desired or lying to get away with something was commonplace in my worldview. If manipulating or lying did not work, I would have a fit of rage as a reaction to not receiving the result I wanted. That is some bad fruit! As God began to produce good fruit in my life, I quickly discovered that I needed to be very intentional about repenting of the rotten fruit and asking his Spirit to remove it from my life. Each time that these bad attributes were removed, I would experience greater joy. The good fruit was being given a healthy environment to become more active and nourishing in my life.

As I began to learn to think on the things (Philippians 4:8) that brought honor to God, they began to renew my mind. I had spent most of my life thinking upon the ways of the world that are contrary to the ways of God. When I got saved, my life looked a bit like a compost bucket of rotten fruit rather than a colorful bowl of fresh sweet fruit. Isn't it wonderful that we have a God who redeems our lives from the pit and turns our ashes into beauty? Or rotten fruit into sweet ripened fruit!

I honestly never believed that my life could become a vessel of honor. But God, in his mercy and grace, puts our lives back on the potter's wheel and reforms us into what his original design for us was intended to be. What joy this brings to the life of the believer! The transformative power of God that restores us to his original intent truly brings "joy unspeakable and full of glory!" (1 Peter 1:8) I love to look at the life of the Apostle Paul, who knew that God had chosen him as a vessel that was so cracked and broken, but he transformed him from Saul to Paul and made something beautiful. This man that had persecuted the believers became the one who became a voice that revealed the depth, heights, width, and lengths of this man we call Jesus.

Day Seven Verse

But the fruit of the Spirit is love, joy, peace, patience, kindness, goodness, faithfulness, gentleness, self-control; against such things there is no law. (Galatians 5:22-23)

DAY SEVEN PRAYER

God, I thank you for your redeeming power that makes my life full of good fruit. Joy is one of the fruits that your Spirit grows in my life, and I am so grateful for this gift. I ask you, Holy Spirit, to come and remove the "rotten fruit" from my life that ruins the good fruit that you are growing in me. Remove the lusts of the flesh, the anxiety, fear, impatience, wickedness, unfaithfulness, harsh ways, and every temptation to control other people. I ask for your ways and the fruit of the Spirit to always be ripe, fresh, and sweet to those around me. Wash me and make me clean so that I may be used as a vessel of honor to declare the beauty of Jesus.

DAY EIGHT
Enter into Joy

When guests come to our front door, I want them to feel as though they've come home. Not merely coming as a visitor but as a member of our family. This is why I intentionally create a welcoming walkway, front porch, and front door. Then, when they enter, I want them greeted with honor, warmth, joy, love, and beauty. I go to great lengths to make every part of our home inviting to all who enter—both physically and spiritually.

One night recently, I woke up hearing the words in my spirit, "Enter in." I saw the beauty of Jesus open like a doorway where people could enter in and be received by the Father, Son, and Holy Spirit. All were welcome, all were wanted, and all were honored within this perfect union of home, family, and love. It was such a place of joy!

> "Come to me, all you who are weary and burdened, and I will give you rest. Take my yoke upon you and learn from me, for I am gentle and humble in heart, and you will find rest for your souls. For my yoke is easy and my burden is light." (Matthew 11:28-30)

Jesus is a refuge, and through him, everyone has a home, a family, and a place of honor at his table. There is no favoritism and no conditions—only acceptance and the invitation to come in—all experience true joy.

Having been raised in a broken home with a lot of chaos and disunity caused me to look for comfort rather than joy. I would do almost anything for comfort because joy seemed so far out of reach. I remember, as a child, being invited into some of my friend's homes where their family made me feel like I was not only welcome— but wanted. They made sure that I knew that "their family was my family." It was in those homes and within those families that I would begin to dream that I, too, could one-day experience joy and have a beautiful family that would be a refuge and hope to all who came in.

One thing that grieves my heart deeply (and grieves the heart of God even more) is when I hear Christians who live gripped in condemnation and fear (not the true fear of the Lord but fear of not being accepted). These individuals often avoid intimacy with God or entering the depths of love that he has invited them into because they feel unworthy or condemned. Yet, this absolutely contradicts who he is! When we believe in Jesus as our Savior and surrender our lives to Him, we are immediately covered and clothed in his righteousness. The filthy, sin-stained garments are removed, and we are clothed in new white garments, garments of mercy and grace through the shed blood and broken body of Jesus. He paid for it all.

Yet, still many remain far off. The beautiful thing is that if you take Jesus at His word and enter in, you will find that his beauty and His righteousness will begin to transform you. Staying outside (afar) and trying to "clean yourself up" will merely take you only as far as your own strength—which is extremely limited— will go. Fighting the flesh with flesh will only take you back to the fallen flesh. But, when you receive—by faith—the white garments of salvation, and enter into Christ as your home, your refuge, then you begin to experience the depth, width, height, and length of his love which is continuously transformational! This is where we go "from glory to glory" as we discover day by day his mercies, his beauty, his wonder, and his love. That is where true change occurs.

> And we, who with unveiled faces all reflect the Lord's glory, are being transformed into His likeness with ever-increasing glory, which comes from the Lord, who is the Spirit. (2 Corinthians 3:18)

Some translations say, "being transformed from glory to glory."

Why are so many believers living with veiled faces—veiled with shame, insecurities, condemnation, and an orphan spirit? When Jesus died on the cross, the veil was torn, and all were invited to enter in through his sacrifice. No longer do we need a high priest to go in for us with a rope tied around his waist in case he is struck dead. Instead, we can enter in through the righteousness of the One who paid the penalty for our sin once and for all! We do not have to keep paying because he paid for it in full.

And by that will, we have been made holy through
the sacrifice of the body of Jesus Christ once for all.
(Hebrews 10:10)

Day Eight Verse

My lips will shout for joy, when I sing praises to you;
my soul also, which you have redeemed.
(Psalm 71:23)

Day Eight Prayer

Thank you, God, that I am no longer condemned, no longer ashamed, no longer far off; and that you invite me to enter your presence with confidence. Jesus, you have clothed me with your righteousness and crowed me with redemption. This truth is a crown of joy for me. Forgive me for the times that I have put back on filthy garments or replaced your crown of joy for a crown of shame and condemnation. I do not want to hold onto these garments any longer. You have removed them as far as the east is from the west, so why do I still look for them? I receive the beautiful, white, and righteous garments that are provided for through the blood of Jesus. I receive your grace and run boldly to come before your throne where I am received with great joy. I receive the crown of joy that you have placed upon my head and I shout for joy, for you have redeemed me!

DAY NINE
Joy in Righteousness

If you talk to most people who have come into the knowledge and commitment of Christ as their Savior, they will share with you the story or testimony of their life before and after Christ. Some of those stories have the details of lives filled with eating, drinking, and being merry. But, they will also tell you that they had to be eating and drinking continuously in order to be merry. Why? Because there was no true joy, and therefore, they turned to alternative forms of filling the empty place within their hearts and lives with temporary substances to alter their reality for a time.

> For the kingdom of God is not a matter of eating and drinking but of righteousness and peace and joy in the Holy Spirit. (Romans 14:17)

I watched this scenario play out in the lives of my parents and many of their friends prior to coming to know the Lord. Usually, after one of their "merry" nights, there would be chaos, fighting, betrayals, and misery. But, that never seemed to stop them from repeating the cycle the next weekend. Yet, when they came to the knowledge and acceptance of Christ as their Savior, they found joy amid peace and righteousness. Going to bed with each night, knowing that they were in right standing with God, gave them peace as their consciences were clear and the unrighteous practices of lying, cheating, and betrayal had ceased.

There is such a joy knowing that we have become citizens of a kingdom where peace and righteousness are foundational. The righteousness of God, in Christ, means that you are justified, declared righteous because you have had your sins cleansed by Jesus.

> "A slave is not a permanent member of the family, but a son belongs to it forever. Therefore, if the Son makes you free, you shall be free indeed."
> (John 8:35-36)

There is such joy in freedom in being set free from the slavery of sin. I have not personally met a single person who has a true joy that is a slave to sin. Jesus, through his death on the cross, emancipated us from the bonds of slavery and brought us into his house (kingdom) as sons. We are permanent members of his family, belonging in his family forevermore. We have an eternal home, an eternal hope, and an eternal right standing that brings us peace and joy.

No longer are we wandering this earth looking for a way to satisfy an insatiable desire to experience joy through means that continue to enslave us to sin. No longer are we acting in ways that bring regret, remorse, and destroy the lives of those that we claim to love. And no longer are we living merely for our time on earth with no hope for eternity. Instead, we have been given a forever home and family in Christ.

What joy—unspeakable joy! We will never be without hope, and we have continual access to peace and joy through the righteousness of Jesus Christ.

Day Nine Verse

You have put more joy in my heart than they have when their grain and wine abound. (Psalm 4:7)

Day Nine Prayer

I cannot thank you enough, Jesus, for setting me free from the slavery of sin and making me a son within your family. I thank you that I can lay down at night with a clear conscience because I am clothed in your righteousness and have received peace and joy through the grace of your salvation. I receive the righteousness of Christ as my robe of sonship. Just as the prodigal son received a ring and a robe from his father when he returned home—declaring him as a son and not a slave—so, I too, receive the ring of covenant and the robe of righteousness that emancipates me from slavery and declares my place as a son. I enter the peace and joy that comes from knowing that by your grace you have set me free. I have hope forevermore—not merely a temporary or circumstantial hope, but an eternal hope that cannot be taken away!

DAY TEN
Restoring Joy

We all have seasons of joy and seasons of pain that we walk through as we journey through this life. I have been through them both, and I have watched people near to me go through them. The mountain top seasons are so beautiful and fulfilling, but the seasons of deep pain can leave a person wondering if they will survive.

One season of pain lasted for three long years. I had known and experienced the most beautiful seasons of joy prior to it, but during that period, I could not even find a glimmer of the joy that I had once knew It began after the birth of my youngest child. It was an exceedingly difficult pregnancy where doctors put me on full bed rest and concluded with a traumatic delivery two months early that almost took the life of both my baby and me. I was plunged into a few years of undiagnosed postpartum depression. It was not until years later that the Lord showed me that the depression had been triggered by this common occurrence after the birth of a child.

The trauma of these near-death experiences caused some deep and undealt with trauma from my childhood to surface. Though I hoped that this painful season would come and go quickly—it did not. In fact, it grew worse with each passing day and month. Those three years were like being held underwater with no air and no one to rescue me. But God, in his great mercy, was there to rescue me. Near the end of this prolonged season of pain, I wondered if I would ever experience joy again. I needed God to restore the joy of my salvation.

One day as our church gathered, I heard the Spirit of God speak to me.

He said, "I am going to rejoice over you with singing and dance for joy because of my love for you."

I did not know what this meant or have much hope of seeing something happen that would restore the joy that I had once experienced. But as worship filled the room, his presence began to wash over me in ways I had forgotten that I could encounter. His love began to touch the deepest parts of my soul.

Then I looked up, and much to my surprise, a group of about six women from our church was dancing in a circle around me. His words, "…I will dance for joy because of my love for you" were demonstrated before me, and I began to weep. As they danced around me, and his love washed over me, the joy of my salvation was restored.

Day Ten Verse

Restore to me the joy of your salvation and uphold me with a willing spirit. (Psalm 51:12)

DAY TEN PRAYER

Jesus, you are my restoration and my hope. I ask you to be the restorer of my joy. Sometimes life has left me empty with despair and fighting to hold onto hope; I am asking you to uphold me by giving me a spirit that is willing to believe again—to hope again. Remind me of the depths of your love and restore to me the unwavering spirit that finds joy in my salvation. I need your presence to wash over me and your love to strengthen me once again. The enemy of my soul has tried to rob me of a willing spirit and of the hope of experiencing joy again. But you alone are my hope and I choose today to receive a hopeful and willing spirit. Thank you for never giving up on me.

DAY ELEVEN
The Fear of the Lord Makes Room for Joy

In my younger years, I dealt with tremendous fear: fear of failure, fear of making the wrong decision, fear of loss, fear of man, and honestly, my biggest fear was the fear of fear. I was more afraid of the repercussions of my weaknesses than I was the awe of God's great ability to protect me and to lead me. I was afraid that my fears or that experiencing one of those fears becoming a reality would cause a reaction from my soul that would grieve God. I feared that I would be like Peter when he denied Christ, forgetting that Peter was not only restored but died for his faith in Christ.

When the Spirit of the Lord began teaching me about what it is to walk in the fear of the Lord, it brought such relief from pressure as I surrendered. Joy and peace replaced the fear and pressure that had plagued my life. According to one source, the fear of the Lord is defined as:

> Fear of God refers to fear or a specific sense of respect, awe, and submission to a deity.

We know that the Word of the Lord is absolute truth and is not to be disputed. Therefore, if we genuinely believe what is written within its pages, then as we understand the promises of God to those who believe, it should leave us in both awe and wonder. What a faithful and loving God who we call "Father." His love, power, authority, judgements, and mercy lead us to a place of awe and respect—even to the point of trembling. As we submit in belief to all that is written in his Word, we find that in that posture of submission and surrender, we find wisdom, knowledge, understanding, and joy.

No longer are we subject to our limited carnal understanding that almost always falls short of true godly wisdom and often comes from a place of limited sight and bad judgement. No, we are no longer tossed around by the fears of our weakness or our bad decisions because we choose to fully submit our plans, thoughts, and lives to the One who has perfect understanding. He is willing and able to lead us in ways that are higher than we understand and to give us wisdom that brings peace, joy, and prosperity.

As part of my ministry, I am blessed to do spiritual counseling. One of the consistent things that I hear in many of my first-time counseling sessions is how so many desire the wisdom of the Lord but do not know how to receive it from him. People tend to put tremendous pressure upon themselves to "hear from God." Yet, the Bible makes it clear that if we ask for wisdom, God is happy to give it to us. The fear of the Lord involves faith that God will make sure he gives us the wisdom that we ask for. We can ask and then rest in the joy that he will answer.

Just the other day, one of my sons was in a dilemma regarding a decision that he needed to make. He was seeking the Lord's wisdom and understanding regarding steps forward. As I was sharing my sense with him, I could see that he was receiving from me, but I could also tell that he was longing for confirmation. The next morning, I unexpectedly came across an article he had written four years earlier. In this article, he explained the dilemma he currently needed God's wisdom for. At the end of his article, he wrote the exact words I had shared with him the day before. This was his confirmation. It was not a still, small voice or a prophetic word, but rather his own words written down on paper four years earlier. God knew that he would need those words later, and sure enough, he made sure that they were heard. When our lives our submitted to the fear of the Lord (his commands and decrees), then we can take joy in the fact that he will make his ways known.

Day Eleven Verse

These are the commands, the decrees and laws the Lord your God directed me to teach you to observe in the land that you are crossing the Jordan to possess, so that you, your children and their children after them may fear the Lord your God as long as you live by keeping all his decrees and commands that I give you, and so that you may enjoy long life.
(Deuteronomy 6:1-2)

Day Eleven Prayer

Father, today I leave behind the fear of failure, the fear of tomorrow, the fear of not hearing your voice along with every other fear. I choose to embrace and live in the fear of the Lord that assures me that wisdom and understanding will follow. I rest in the joy of your promises and your mercy to lead me in the everlasting way. From this day onward I will trust you to lead me and to guide me in the way I should go. My ways are not your ways for they always lead me astray. I put my faith in the promise that you will give me wisdom in each and every step that I take. What a great joy it is to be free of the pressure of having to figure out the way forward.

DAY TWELVE
Joy in Stillness

One of the greatest gifts in my life has been learning the gift of stillness. It is a grace that comes as we enter a deep and abiding faith in God's watchful care over our lives. I did not grow up with a father that watched over me with the protective care that children need; therefore, I had learned to take care of myself (which was more destructive than helpful). However, our heavenly Father does not miss a detail and is a constant presence in the life of his sons and daughters.

Most believers struggle with stillness more than any other thing. This world teaches us to watch our backs, protect our hearts, and not trust others with the details of our lives. The Holy Spirit gently leads us into a new way of living that lets down our guards and opens our hearts to trust God even in difficult circumstances. For many of us, this is a difficult place of surrender. Yet, when we close the door on a life of worry and self-protection and open our lives to trust and stillness, it makes room for incredible joy.

> "Therefore, do not worry, saying, 'What shall we eat?' or 'What shall we drink?' or 'What shall we wear?' For the Gentiles strive after all these things, and your heavenly Father knows that you need them. But seek first the kingdom of God and His righteousness, and all these things will be added unto you. Therefore, do not worry about tomorrow, for tomorrow will worry about itself. Each day has enough trouble of its own." (Matthew 6:32-34)

Worrying about tomorrow depletes today's joy. Joy and worry are like oil and water—they do not mix. When I began yielding to the nurturing love of the Holy Spirit, he began to renew my mind and to teach me a new way of living. My racing mind came into a stillness and trust that made room for an abundant life. As I watched his faithfulness make a way in the wilderness of this world for supernatural provision and comfort, I began to experience peace, love, and joy. Truly knowing that there is a God who cares for his children draws us into such comfort and joy.

God's presence and constant care do not mean that we will no longer face hardships or trials during our journey through life. The Bible assures us that we will face tribulations in this world, but we are to be of good cheer because Jesus has overcome the world. We must be reminded by James 1:2-4, which says that our trials produce endurance, endurance produces character, and character produces hope in the glory of God. My son-in-law, Luke, one day said, "The pressures of life brought me to the place of alignment with God, and that alignment was surrender." As we surrender our control or dependency on self, we embrace trust and confidence in a God who never leaves or forsakes us.

The journey may have challenges, trials, and pain, but there is a faithful Father who has given us an eternal hope that ushers in joy.

Day Twelve Verse

He says, "Be still, and know that I am God; I will be exalted among the nations, I will be exalted in the earth." (Psalm 46:10)

Day Twelve Prayer

Holy Spirit, today I want to begin the journey into stillness. I give you all my worries, my self-reliance, my fears and my anxious thoughts. I know that I have a faithful Father who is ever-present. God, watch over every detail of my life to assure that I have joy on the journey to my eternal hope. I ask you to help me when the pressures of life come to surrender all of my fretting in exchange for the abiding stillness of trust. I ask you to teach me the grace of stillness that knows that you are God!

DAY THIRTEEN
The Joyful Dance

I always love the saying, "Joy comes in the morning." Sorrows come and bring us into a dark night of the soul, but there is a promise of joy that comes with a new day. For the believer, even death is followed by the greatest joy we will ever know. Joy has the final word in our lives.

The dance of joy often breaks the heavy yoke of oppression. The dance of victory is surely filled with joy- like when Miriam danced as her people crossed the Red Sea out of the captivity of Egypt or as David danced when the Ark of the Lord was brought back into Israel. But, there is a dance that awakens our souls to joy in the middle of the darkness. I remember a time in my life where a season of darkness had come upon me, and I wondered if I would see the light of day again. Then, one day, I looked at the darkness around me, and I knew that it was time to get above it. Suddenly, I was given the strength to get up and dance. I danced on that darkness with the fullness of joy. I grabbed hold of the joy of the Lord and let it fill me with hope, with strength, and with light. There are times to grieve and mourn, but there are times to take hold of the joy of the Lord and let it become our strength.

> The Lord is my strength and shield. I trust him with all my heart. He helps me, and my heart is filled with joy. I burst out in songs of thanksgiving.
> (Psalm 28:7)

His joy is not only our strength, but it is also our shield. His joy protects our hearts from despair and aligns us with the truth that we are not without help, and his help fills us with joy and thanksgiving. We are promised that nothing can separate us from his love, and this is the greatest joy of all. His love is ever-present when we feel joy as well as in the times when we choose joy. Yes, there are times that we need to choose joy in the midst of sorrows.

Joy can also be called "delight." Psalm 37:4 says, "Delight yourself in the Lord, and he will give you the desires of your heart." Delight, or being joyful in the Lord, releases the fulfillment of the desires of your heart. The greatest thing that I have discovered is that delighting in him is truly the deepest desire of my heart. We were created to delight in him as he delights in us.

> For the LORD your God is living among you. He is a mighty savior. He will take delight in you with gladness. With his love, he will calm all your fears. He will rejoice over you with joyful songs.
> (Zephaniah 3:17)

We are his delight, his great joy! And in turn, he has become our delight and the greatest joy that we will ever know.

Day Thirteen Verse

You have turned my mourning into joyful dancing.
You have taken away my clothes of mourning and clothed me with joy,
that I might sing praises to you and not be silent.
O LORD my God, I will give you thanks forever!
(Psalm 30:11-12)

DAY THIRTEEN PRAYER

Today I choose joy! There is joy in your presence and pleasures for me forevermore. You are my helper, my protector (shield), my strength in weakness, and my light in the darkness. You show me the way forward and cause my feet to dance for joy. I choose today to shake off sorrows and burst beyond the darkness into your great light. I even have hope beyond the grave that gives me eternal joy. I am your delight and you have become my delight through every season and step in my life.

DAY FOURTEEN
The Blood Brings Joy

The blood of our precious Savior has provided an eternal hope that brings us great joy as we go through this journey of life. His blood paid the price to redeem us from sin and death, securing a new covenant between God and man. No trial, no circumstance, and no man can separate us from what his blood has provided.

> You have come to Jesus, the one who mediates the new covenant between God and people, and to the sprinkled blood, which speaks (a better word) of forgiveness instead of crying out for vengeance like the blood of Abel. (Hebrews 12:24)

Jesus is the mediator of this new covenant—we must go through him to enter in. We go through the blood that joins us together with God, and no man can separate us from what he has provided. This is the truth that fills our hearts and lives with unspeakable joy. It is a joy that remains through every moment and day of our lives. This is the joy that we want the whole world to know that they have been invited into. This is what Jesus died for.

If you have entered this new covenant through Christ, then you have been given the gift of joy. The joy of the Lord is your strength. You have entered a life filled with hope, promise, inheritance, and love. Mankind was never meant to live separated from this truth and invitation. We were never supposed to be separated from God through the trespasses of our sin. The blood of Jesus has made way for all things to be made new again.

This is a joy that is unshakable. It is a joy that goes beyond our emotions and into the truth of our eternal promise. Not even death can rob us of this joy. I remember my life before coming to the knowledge of salvation through Jesus. I spent every day looking for momentary joy, which, when found, was short-lived and fleeting. I searched for companionship and acceptance, but what I really wanted was love. I had experienced the selfish love that man offers, but I longed for a love that I had never heard of: *agape* love. It was *agape* love that caused the Father to send His Son, to shed His blood, which turned our mourning into joy.

When Jesus left his disciples, the blood he had shed made way for their joy to be complete. From that point on, they had full access to the Father, Son, and Holy Spirit through the name of Jesus. By his blood and in his name our joy has been made complete.

Day Fourteen Verse

"Until now you have not asked for anything in my name. Ask and you will receive, and your joy will be complete." (John 16:24)

Day Fourteen Prayer

Today I enter into the joy that you died for, Jesus. Forgive me for not recognizing the fullness of joy that your blood provided for me. It is a joy that overcomes even death. No man can separate me from it and no pain can deplete its power to strengthen me. I receive the revelation of your joy and how it completes me. I am never left without help and will never again experience separation from you. I declare over my life that the joy of the Lord is my strength and my song!

DAY FIFTEEN
Fellowship With Joy

> Because your lovingkindness is better than life, My lips shall praise You. Thus I will bless You while I live, I will life up my hands in Your name, My soul shall be satisfied as with marrow and fatness, And my mouth shall praise You with joyful lips.
> (Psalm 63: 3-4)

I have some lifelong friendships that have given me many of my favorite times of fellowship. These are friends that know me so intimately—they know my strengths and celebrate them, and they know my weaknesses and surround me with their strength in those areas and moments where weakness causes me pain. Fellowship with them is sweet, and it is safe. I experience great joy through true friendship.

Through the years, there have been many times that our family no longer lived near these precious friends. Though they are but a phone call away, I could not always stop to call them. When I had gone through times of loneliness or pain and did not have access to one of my faithful friends,

I knew that I had Jesus. Yet, have you ever had moments where even Jesus felt far off and as if you could not gain access to enter fellowship with him? I am certain that we all have experienced that. Though it is merely a feeling (not ever our reality), it still can cause us to feel stuck and alone.

One of the ways that I have discovered a direct pathway into fellowship with Jesus is through joy. I have learned that when sorrow wants to partner with my soul, I can enter into "fellowship with joy," and it becomes a pathway to his experiential presence.

Philippians 4: 8 has been great wisdom to taking me into a time of fellowship with joy.

> Finally, brothers and sisters, whatever is true, whatever is noble, whatever is right, whatever is pure, whatever is lovely, whatever is admirable—if anything is excellent or praiseworthy—think about such things.

As I begin to put these words of wisdom into practice, I enter into what I describe as my "fellowship with joy." Joy becomes my faithful friend who always speaks what is true, what is noble, what is right, what is pure, what is lovely, what is admirable, and what is praiseworthy. As I begin to turn my thoughts and mind toward these things, joy and peace are restored. Joy is like that friend who always has words of encouragement and wisdom when you need it most. Joy never is inaccessible or unobtainable. Some days it is a choice to let joy in and begin to fellowship with her. But how grateful I am when I do. Sorrow desires to isolate me from fellowship with God and with others, but joy takes me by the hand and invites me in.

Next time you are feeling sad or lonely—or even far from God—take the hand of joy and let those praiseworthy things fill your mind and pour forth from your mouth. Watch how quickly you will come into his presence with praise as you choose fellowship with joy.

Day Fifteen Verse

The joy of the LORD is your strength.
(Nehemiah 8:10)

Day Fifteen Prayer

Jesus, today I choose to enter into fellowship with joy! I refuse to take the hand of sorrow, depression, or loneliness, but I will take the hand of joy and let it lead me to into Your presence. I shift my thoughts from things that are downcast to things that are praiseworthy and true. I receive joy as a faithful friend who is near and who speaks truth and the right perspective to me. I yield my soul to walk with joy even when sorrow pulls upon me to walk down its path. I know that joy will lead me to you and your joy. Your joy is my strength and my song in every season.

DAY SIXTEEN
Joy is Healing

Joy is like medicine for our souls! Have you ever experienced such a long, deep laugh that, when it was finished, you felt released from pain and anguish? I am convinced that this is why the Holy Spirit will visit people with the manifestation of laughter—it is healing, it is contagious, and it is a deep infusion of joy.

> A joyful heart is good medicine, but a crushed spirit dries up the bones. (Proverbs 17:22)

The enemy seeks to crush our spirits because it makes us brittle and vulnerable to being broken. That is why the Bible says that the joy of the Lord is our strength. We can ask the Holy Spirit to restore a joyful spirit to us because it will be medicine to our souls. Joy heals, and joy strengthens our inward being.

> Create in me a pure heart, oh, God, and renew your right Spirit within me. (Psalm 51:10)

What is a "right Spirit"? I believe it is a right attitude or proper perspective that is aligned with pure truth. It is having joy deep within our spirits—deep within our inward parts. One version of Psalm 51:10 reads like this:

> Create in me a clean heart, O God; and renew a right spirit in my inward parts.

Joy is like a healing balm or rushing water that cleanses us from the infection of being crushed in spirit. We know that we all face times of pain and grieving, but we cannot live there or make our home there because it will dry us up. I believe that deep sorrows that are not met with the conclusion of joy cause our bodies to become sick and vulnerable to disease. I am not saying that this is the root of disease; I am merely suggesting that a crushed spirit that does not eventually receive the "morning of joy" weakens a person in their body, soul, and spirit. There are times that it is not as simple as "choosing joy," and we must reach out to both the Holy Spirit and to the body of Christ to surround us with prayer. We can ask for his people to lay hands on us and heal us from a crushed spirit. I have had seasons in my life that I had to do this, and there is no shame in needing help.

Often within the church walls, there is a sense of shame or harsh judgement if someone is crushed in spirit. Just as there are times when we need a doctor's assistance to deal with a physical ailment, it is true that we need the family of God to assist us with an emotional or spiritual ailment such as depression or unbearable sorrow. My sister-in-law recently lost her husband (my brother) to Covid. I have watched her reach out to friends to surround her, pray for her, weep with her, and laugh with her. It is good medicine in this time of deep grief and loss. It is not weakness to have sorrow or pain, but if it is not given the doses of joy, it will harm the person going through it.

I wish we could take joy like a daily vitamin that we pop in our mouth and swallow with water, but it is not that simple. We do need it to heal us and strengthen us each day, but it often comes in the form of a friend, song, or an encouraging word. If you know someone going through grief or depression, reach out to them and ask the Holy Spirit what you can bring as a dose of joy to infuse their inward parts with healing.

Restore unto me, the joy of my salvation…and renew a right spirit within me.

Day Sixteen Verse

A time to weep, and a time to laugh; a time to mourn, and a time to dance… (Ecclesiastes 3:4)

Day Sixteen Prayer

Lord, help me to understand the times and seasons of my life. I know that weeping comes, but I know that laughter must follow. I know that mourning comes, but dancing must come to my steps once again. Joy is healing, and laughter is medicine, so today, I ask you to give me the joy that heals and the laughter that is medicine to my soul. Heal me of any place that I am crushed in spirit and bring me joy once again. I choose joy, and I desire laughter! Put a right spirit within me.

DAY SEVENTEEN
Comfort and Joy

All of us have experienced the joy of eating what we call comfort food. It is usually warm, savory, rich, and it tastes like home. It feels like your grandma cooked you a meal on a rainy day that brings comfort to your mouth and stomach with the flavor of her love. The Holy Spirit loves to come and set before you a meal of the finest spiritual foods to comfort you and bring you joy.

> "I give you all the freshest olive oil and all the finest new wine and grain that the Israelites give to the LORD as their firstfruits." (Numbers 18:12)

You are not supposed to be like a dog that eats the crumbs from the master's table. You were created to feast upon the finest of foods from his heavenly storehouse. You have been invited to dine at his table each day, not as a guest, but as a son or a daughter. Although it is not healthy to eat the comfort foods of this earth on a daily basis, it is absolutely healthy and well-advised to eat the food of heaven that comforts, nourishes, and strengthens you in your inward parts.

The Holy Spirit is like that loving grandmother who welcomes you into the warmth of her home and sits you down to a homecooked meal that was baked with thoughtfulness and love. Each day you are invited by the Comforter, who feeds you with truth, revelation, love, and refreshing nourishment. What he serves you, when ingested into your soul and spirit, brings you a deep, abiding joy that surpasses circumstances and even human understanding. It goes beyond the flesh, right to your soul and spirit, to comfort you with a joy only known to those who love God and are called by his name.

We all need comfort. We need it not only in times of pain but also at the end of a long day or after going through a time of transition when things are unfamiliar. One of my personal favorite expressions of comfort is long, sincere hugs that, without words, speak to my soul a thousand words of tender love. They are deeply comforting to me, and they settle me when things around me feel unsettled. I also thrive on words of affirmation—especially from my family. I love deeply; therefore, I have a need to be loved deeply and affectionately in return. Unfortunately, because a lot of my family lives thousands of miles away from where God has my husband and I currently serving, I do not get many of these embraces or words of affirmation. Yet, the Holy Spirit is with me every moment of every day. He knows when I need a spiritual embrace, a word of affirmation, or a spiritual meal that will refresh me and warm my heart.

And he knows when you need comfort as well.

The result of being comforted is to be reconnected with the abiding joy that comes from the all-surpassing love of Jesus.

One of the most amazing things about being comforted is that we can pass it on to others who need comfort. The Bible says that we "comfort with the comfort that we have been given."

> Praise be to the God and Father of our Lord Jesus Christ, the Father of compassion and the God of all comfort, who comforts us in all our troubles, so that we can comfort those in any trouble with the comfort we ourselves receive from God. For just as we share abundantly in the sufferings of Christ, so also our comfort abounds through Christ.
> (2 Corinthians 1:3-5)

As Christians, we all share abundantly in the sufferings of Christ (probably more than we realize), but the Father of compassion and the God of all comfort is with us. He is with us to comfort us in all our afflictions, troubles, and pain. As we experience his compassion and comfort, we then have compassion upon others and can comfort them in their sorrows and troubles. As I am writing this book on joy, I have been facing one of the hardest times of pain in many years. Four months ago, I lost my only brother to Covid. He had overcome lymphoma only six months previously, and was celebrating the victory with his family, friends, and church with tremendous joy. At Christmas time, he tested positive for Covid, and by New Year's Eve 2020, he was struggling to breathe. He was admitted to the hospital. Twenty-one days later, life support was removed, and he entered eternal joy.[1]

Those of us left behind, especially his wife, were in great need of God's comfort and the comfort of those who love us. There were days that the grief was so deep that I felt like I could not breathe, but the Holy Spirit would come and comfort me, and in turn, I had the capacity to reach out and comfort his wife and children with the comfort I had received. Everything that we receive from the Lord can be passed on to another. We are one in him—so what is his is ours, and what is ours also belongs to our brothers and sisters.

Compassion and comfort are far more contagious than any deadly virus. It is a life-giving gift to receive comfort and to give comfort. What a joy it is to know that we are never left to live this life apart from compassion or comfort. The Comforter lives within us and is always available to give us all that we need.

---

[1] For more of the story, see my book *Finding Home*.

Day Seventeen Verse

"So do not fear, for I am with you;
do not be dismayed, for I am your God.
I will strengthen you and help you;
I will uphold you with my righteous right hand."
(Isaiah 41:10)

DAY SEVENTEEN PRAYER

Holy Spirit, I turn to you for comfort and compassion in my day of trouble. I know that your people face many afflictions, but you came as our Comforter to sustain us, heal us, and to restore our joy. I cannot move through afflictions without your comfort, and I cannot comfort others without first experiencing your comfort for myself. I accept your invitation to come and sit with you as you comfort me. I receive the nourishment of your comfort, the affirmation of your love, and the abiding joy of your faithfulness to me.

DAY EIGHTEEN
Joy in the Little Things

We all have days that are what we'd call mediocre. They are not terrible, but they would not be considered outstanding. Far more days are mediocre than one of the other extremes. The normal days make room for the highs or the lows. On these days, I try to always find something to find joy in. Of course, we always have joy in the awareness of our salvation and God's love for us, but I try to find moments that I seek out something that brings my heart joy.

These moments are like God's breath that comes to refresh me and to bring a little burst of joy to my soul. Often, I must intentionally stop my activity and take time to find something that causes my heart to be glad. For me, it can be remembering to step outside and watch the sunset or stop to admire some aspect of God's beautiful creation. It can even be a moment playing with our pup or enjoying a shared meal with my husband.

It is good to nurture our souls! If we do not take the time to care for our souls, then we will begin to burn out. For Jeff, it is sitting down with a good book or watching one of his favorite guy movies. For one of my sons, it is playing his guitar or fixing something (even if it doesn't need fixing); for one of my daughters, it is found in singing or writing music, and for another son, it is having time together with family.

Whatever nurtures your soul, make sure that you take the time to do it. I talk to Christians often who do not take time to rest or nurture their souls. They pray, read the Word, worship, work, minister, and serve, but they have forgotten how to nurture their souls. It is not unspiritual to find joy in the things that move your heart and bring you entertainment. As a matter of fact, it is necessary for your physical, emotional, and spiritual health. I rarely hear a sermon on having fun, and yet, it is what many Christians need to stop and do. Yes, we need to pray, worship, study the Bible, and serve, but we also need to be refreshed and enjoy life, also. We need to stop each day and nurture the experience of joy, if even for a moment.

In all my years of travel and ministry, this is what I see lacking in those who are in leadership within the church. God did not make such a beautifully detailed world around us only to have it go unnoticed by the busyness of our schedules. I love to enjoy the journey rather than just get to the destination.

I often say to my kids or my young grandkids how kind it was of God to make animals such as a sloth or a baby goat. Why? Because they make you giggle with joy. Why does a sloth move so slow with the very same look you saw on your husband's face that morning as he struggled to get out of bed? Why does a baby goat jump like he has springs in his feet and makes a shockingly loud crying noise that makes anyone near laugh uncontrollably? Because it brings God joy and he knew that it would bring us joy.

This is why animal Instagram posts or videos have so many views! They bring joy to our souls. They may be the "little things," but God is in the little things, and joy is found in these little things. Don't ignore them; and if you have been, retrain yourself to stop and take notice of them. Stop and take time to nurture joy. It's like a daily vitamin for your soul's health.

Day Eighteen Verse

When I consider your heavens,
the work of your fingers,
the moon and the stars,
which you have set in place,
what is mankind that you are mindful of them,
human beings that you care for them?
(Psalm 8:3-4)

Day Eighteen Prayer

God, I am going to stop today to consider the work of your hands because you put so much beauty and joy around us. I am sorry that I have rushed by so many of your fingerprints that you put in my path to nurture my soul. Today I will intentionally begin to take time to do something that brings me joy or consider something seemingly insignificant that makes me smile or even laugh. My soul needs to experience the many forms of joy you put here on earth because you care for us. Thank you for all these things that are gifts from your hand for my life. I will find joy in the little things and take the time to truly let them nurture my soul.

Day Nineteen
The Joy of Fellowship

Aren't friendships wonderful gifts? I have had one friend who has been what I would call a "best friend" for almost forty years! I know this is rare, but somehow, we have shared this uncommon gift. We met when I was eighteen, and we were as different as any two people could be. Our only common ground was our ages, our church, and that we both loved Jesus. But, I knew that Jesus said that we were to be friends. We double-dated our "soon to be" spouses (who were also best friends), we were at the births of each other's children, we homeschooled our kids together, we have taken hundreds of "nights out" together, and shared thousands of conversations.

We have also cared for one another when one was hurting and wept when one was grieving—and we had sat in silence when we just needed someone nearby. For the past decade, I've lived far away from her, but we have made time to travel and visit one another (even when we lived in another country). There is nothing I cannot tell her and nothing she can't tell me. That is true fellowship.

Because our family has moved and traveled so much for ministry purposes, I have now made friends all over the world—some are casual friends, and some have become trusted, deep friends. No matter where we have lived, I make sure that I seek out finding one or two friendships that I can not only share my faith with, but that I can share my life with.

I don't like pretenses or having to wear masks, so I need people that I can be vulnerable and real with. Performance-driven relationships wear me out, so I gravitate to those who I can be real with. I love being with people who will strengthen me in my weaknesses (be willing to see them and help me with them) and let me strengthen them in their weaknesses. I call time spent in these relationships true fellowship. They are the people that will be there when you are not at your best, when you are sick, or when you are hurting. These are the friends that celebrate your joys and your accomplishments and don't shy away in jealousy or competition. These are the friends that truly bring joy to your soul. These friendships are found by those looking for hidden treasures; they are rare and priceless.

Finding true, deep, and lasting fellowship will bring great joy in your life. But, deep friendships begin with acquaintances who are willing to invest time and vulnerability. No one becomes a trusted friend apart from taking the time and effort required to build trust. God created us for connection with others, and he wired us to shine brighter when we are in connection. Joy comes from the fellowship that brings true and lifelong friendships.

We have fellowship and friendship with Jesus—which also was built over time as we learned to put our trust in him. Salvation begins the journey of friendship with our Lord, but it only comes with invested time and a willingness to walk in vulnerability with him. Many experience salvations but few become true friends with him. But for the few who do, oh what joy is experienced.

Day Nineteen Verse

I thank my God every time I remember you. In all my prayers for all of you, I always pray with joy because of your partnership in the gospel from the first day until now, being confident of this, that he who began a good work in you will carry it on to completion until the day of Christ Jesus.
(Philippians 1:3-6)

Day Nineteen Prayer

Lord, I recognize that the true and deep friendships that will bring me joy begin with fellowship. I want to be counted among your friends and I want to nurture friendships with those who you have placed in my life. I choose to commit to spend time with others and to be honest and vulnerable with them. I will love others, listen to their joys and pains, be there in joy and sorrow, strengthen them in their weaknesses without judgments and celebrate their accomplishments. It is my joy to be a friend of God and a friend to those you love.

DAY TWENTY
Joy Washes Over Me

This life can be hard. Sometimes it seems that the hard is more frequent than the ease. It was not supposed to be this way, but when sin entered the world, labor and death touched everything. One day, Jesus will change all of this when h returns and sets up his kingdom on earth. Every tear will be wiped away, and death will be no more—joy will wash over every sorrow.

We do not have to wait for joy to wash over us because through Christ, we have entered our eternal inheritance. Yes, we still have sufferings to face and struggles to wrestle with, but the joy of the Lord becomes our strength and washes over us when we need it the most.

I remember a season when my husband was facing a time of struggling with weariness and discouragement. He was overcome by so much of the evil that he viewed around the world. One evening we were at a special church service together; he was feeling especially discouraged; the burdens were weighing heavily upon his heart. During the service, the joy of the Lord hit the congregation, and laughter broke out throughout the building. The laughter only made the pain that he was experiencing worse. Suddenly he found himself lying on the floor crying out to God while everyone around him laughed uncontrollably.

As he lay there, he was asking God hard questions. Questions like, "What are you going to do about the starving children in the world?" and "What are you going to do about the evil that is destroying families?"

To each of the questions, Jeff heard the Spirit of the Lord laugh and say, *"Son, I know exactly what I am going to do about that."*

It was like God was slapping his leg in confident joy as he answered him. As this happened, joy would sweep over him and wash the pain and burdens away. By the time his questioning was over, he was laughing with such deep joy and was set free from the season of struggling.

Did you know that God has an answer for every question that you have? Did you know that he knows exactly what he's going to do about that burden that you've been carrying? The answer may seem delayed, but his timing is perfect, his ways are perfect and is wisdom is above all other's counsel. You can cast all your cares upon him and know that he has the answer. You don't have to carry it because he will carry it for you. Just like when a parent sees their child carrying something that is too heavy for them, they will stop and carry it for them, so it is with our God.

It is time to release the burden and let joy wash over you anew. Release the pain, the worries, the nagging questions, and the striving to find answers—release it all to him. Let his laughter and his joy flow like a river through your weary soul and be refreshed by his living water.

> On the last and greatest day of the festival, Jesus stood and said in a loud voice, "Let anyone who is thirsty come to me and drink. Whoever believes in me, as Scripture has said, rivers of living water will flow from within them." (John 7:37)

Our burdens, which were never ours to carry alone, merely cause the flow of the living waters to be blocked. As we release them to the Lord, his waters are unstopped and begin to flow, becoming rivers of joy that cause us to skip in freedom and delight.

Day Twenty Verse

The One enthroned in heaven laughs;
the Lord scoffs at them.
He rebukes them in his anger
and terrifies them in his wrath, saying,
"I have installed my king
on Zion, my holy mountain."
(Psalm 2:4-6)

Day Twenty Prayer

Lord, today I cast my cares upon you! I take all the questions, burdens, worries and things that are out of my control and I let you carry them for me. You have every answer for every question and every prayer. You know what you are going to do about every circumstance and situation that I face. So, I give them all to you. Unstop the flow of your living water that brings me joy. Unstop the fountain of life that raises me up from a low place. When I cannot figure out an answer, I will enter the joy of knowing that you have every answer to every question known to man. You are King and I invite your joy to wash over me and sweep all my cares away.

DAY TWENTY-ONE
Joyful Expectation

Did you know that in many instances in the Bible, the word "hope" can be translated to mean joyful expectation? To lose hope is to lose faith because as Hebrews 11:1 says,

> Now faith is the assurance of what we hope for and
> the certainty of what we do not see.

It is not only good, but essential to our souls to have joyful expectations for our life here and now. God has given each of us dreams, desires, and hopes that bring us great joy as we expect their fulfillment. Someone who is very close to me has been facing a decade of infertility, and I stand in continuous joyful expectation that she and her husband will conceive a child. Together, we dream about this little promise; we have talked about it, bought items to prepare for it, she and her husband have picked out names; plans have been made in joyful expectation. This does not mean that there are not many tears, frustrations, disappointments—even the desire to stop hoping. But, hope continues, and this hope produces joyful expectation even amid deep heartache for them.

My husband and I also faced years of infertility, so I know the rollercoaster of joyful expectation, only to be met by painful disappointments. The day that I held our adopted eleven-month-old daughter in my arms for the first time, I experienced a complete release from all the sorrows that came from the years of "hope deferred." Then, less than a year later, I held my infant son, who I gave birth to.

We are not guaranteed that every hope that we have will be fulfilled on this side of heaven, but we do have a guarantee that the hope in our eternal promise will be fulfilled. Whether or not we see every fulfillment of hopes and dreams come to pass, it is still essential to live in the place of joyful expectation. It is life to our souls and health to our hearts.

The dreams that children have of becoming an astronaut or ballerina or fireman nurture imagination and joyful expectation. Though they may never actually ride in a rocket ship, this joyful childhood dream is necessary for their growth and for nurturing their hope in the unseen. We were created to dream big in joyful expectation. If we could retain this childlike posture, it would truly break off the posturing of settling for something less than God's best for us.

> Now to Him who is able to do immeasurably more than all we ask or imagine, according to His power that is at work within us, to Him be glory in the church and in Christ Jesus throughout all generations, for ever and ever! Amen. (Ephesians 3:20-21)

Often, we stop believing in the "more than we can ask or imagine." Yet, children are proof that we are to dream of bigger thingsthan what we have been able to imagine. I have rarely met a young child with small dreams—they have not been subject to all the things we learn that cause us to limit our dreams by carnal knowledge.

Common sense can be a great enemy of dreams, but the wisdom of God causes us to enter a joyful expectation of seeing "Him who is able" to do more than we can ask or imagine. I truly believe that the quenching of joyful expectation through common sense or man's wisdom is more dangerous to the human soul than most any other thing.

> "Which of you, if your son asks for bread, will give him a stone? Or if he asks for a fish, will give him a snake? If you, then, though you are evil, know how to give good gifts to your children, how much more will your Father in heaven give good gifts to those who ask him!" (Matthew 7:9-11)

Shouldn't we dream of flying rockets or bringing healing to the sick? Shouldn't we renew the areas of joyful expectation that have been diluted by the wisdom of men? Yes!

When my husband and I began the journey to adopt our oldest daughter, we were young and so full of joyful expectation that we said yes to a journey that was "impossible" in the eyes of men. The chances of us adopting this baby girl were truly impossible in the natural realm—judges told us that we did not have a prayer, social workers told us that there was no way for us to become her parents, and even Christians looked at us as if we were a desperate young couple immature and foolish in our faith and hope. Yet, I had heard my Father's voice say, "Trust me and go forth in faith."

Numerous times along the path, we hit walls that confirmed the natural impossibility we were facing, but the Father continued to say, "Only believe." Nine months later, by unheard-of miracles and out of the faith of joyful expectation, we held her in our arms and took her home as our daughter.

I often wonder if God asked the same thing today (thirty years later), would I be as quick to give my yes? Have I "matured" to the point that I have lost the joyful expectation that would venture on such an impossible journey with the hope of God fulfilling what he spoke to my heart? Have I matured in the ways of the world, in human understanding, in what we call "common sense?"

May it never be so!

It is time for us to return to the God "who is able to do above and beyond all that we can ask or imagine" and enter the childlike, joyful expectation that we had when we first began walking with him.

Day Twenty-one Verse

And by faith even Sarah, who was past childbearing age, was enabled to bear children because she considered him faithful who had made the promise.
(Hebrews 11:11)

Day Twenty-one Prayer

Father, today I ask you to restore the childlike faith and joyful expectation to me. I declare that every place in my heart and soul that has become diluted by common sense or the wisdom of men would not receive a full restoration of hope and joy. I proclaim today that you are the God who is able to do more than I can ask or imagine! I will not settle for less than the miraculous. I will no longer limit my dreams, because that has diluted my joy and expectation of greater things.

DAY TWENTY-TWO
Joy is a Key

We all have seasons of hardship and even grieving, but they must come to an end. If the hard seasons linger beyond when they should, often it will impact our minds and emotions in ways that begin to cause damage. This happens when we take matters into our own hands and try to control the uncontrollable pain that comes upon us during these times. There is a surrender that must happen in wilderness seasons where we let go of our will and our control and let him do all that he desires to do. His desire is to heal us, restore us and give us back all that has been lost.

> Therefore, I am now going to allure her; I will lead her into the wilderness and speak tenderly to her. There I will give her back her vineyards and will make the Valley of Achor (Trouble) a door of hope. There she will respond as in the days of her youth, as in the day she came up out of Egypt.
> (Hosea 2:14-15)

Your season of trouble is designed as a door of hope for you to cross through. The joyful expectation that you declared in the past pages will prove to be a key to open this door of hope. Even in pain, you can have joyful expectation and use it as key to open that door of hope. This is your partnership with Jesus as he walks you from the valley of trouble to the breakthrough into abundant living. The hope of joy becomes the hand that holds the key and reaches to the keyhole, and on the other side of the door is a joy that revives you to true living.

You cannot let go of the hope of experiencing great joy again during times of sorrow. Emotions are a large part of every person, and though we cannot allow them to control us or control our truth—we still need to experience the emotions that joy brings. We need to laugh long and hard, we need to have moments of awe and wonder, and we need to feel deep and lasting love. These are the things that heal the emotional trauma of things that we experience as we walk this journey of life. Joy always is like healing balm on the wounds of pain. So, laugh, dance, behold, and love. Joy is the key to healing and life.

Day Twenty-two Verse

A time to weep, and a time to laugh; a time to mourn and a time to dance.
(Ecclesiastes 3:4)

Day Twenty-two Prayer

God, I will recognize the times and seasons of my life, and I will hold the key to joy during the seasons of sorrow that will open the door of hope for me. I will be purposeful about making time to laugh, making time to "stand in awe," and making time to dance. Though there are hard seasons, I will rejoice and celebrate greatly during the seasons of joy. You are my reason for hope and my joy through each and every season of life.

DAY TWENTY-THREE
The Still Waters of Joy

The very first portion of scripture that I ever read was the 23rd Psalm. The first time I read the words of this psalm, it was like being washed by the words; they washed away the hopelessness and covered me with a joy that I had never experienced. My life had been filled with turbulent waters, so to be led to still waters was like a baptism in peace and joy.

This was the very first place that the Lord led me in my journey with him. He knew it was where I would be able to inhale deeply and take a few moments just to allow his presence to fill the space of my soul. During that time, I was not experiencing an emotional joy that took the form of laughter or dancing—what I experienced was the first taste of abiding joy that is deep and still. It was like a long, healing embrace.

There is a constant invitation before every son and daughter of God to let the Good Shepherd lead you to green pastures and still waters. This is your abiding place where a joy that is deep and wide is imparted to you. This is the place where you can go in every season, and every journey life brings you to. If you do not allow time in the still places, then you will not know where to go when the waters around you become turbulent. This will always be the place where you will find the "eye of the storm." I call it home base. We all need a home base where we find safety and embrace.

When my youngest son was a little boy, our family moved to another country. We moved away from his home, his friends, his cousins, and his grandparents. He was just under seven years old and somehow thought that we were just going on a visit, and when he realized that we were not going home, he began to cling to me everywhere we went. For him, I was his still waters, his eye of the storm, and his home base. That was okay when he was a boy, but when he grew up, he had to re-establish his home base in his relationship with Jesus. I think that was a tough transition (for us both), but each of us is responsible for finding and establishing that inner place with Christ. If we don't, we will always turn to things that are temporal or fleeting—things that can be shaken or removed. I may not always be there for my son, but Jesus will be, and that place of stillness with his Prince of Peace will always invite him home.

Have you established your abiding place deep in your soul? The Holy Spirit is there to help you find home and stillness. It is good to form a habit of visiting the still waters at some point each and every day. It is there that your soul is renewed, and your mind is transformed. For me, it is where I go in my "secret place" time—where I get still and listen for his whisper and find his hand to hold mine. I can recalibrate and realign my heart and thoughts with his at the edge of the still waters, and I find abiding joy in this place.

Day Twenty-three Verse

"As the Father has loved me, so have I loved you. Now remain in my love. If you keep my commands, you will remain in my love, just as I have kept my Father's commands and remain in his love. I have told you this so that my joy may be in you and that your joy may be complete." John 15:9-11

Day Twenty-three Prayer

Jesus, you are my shepherd, and you are the only one who can lead me beside those still waters that restore my soul and give me joy. I never want to run ahead of you or forsake the invitation to come and sit with you in the stillness of your presence. I know that in your presence is fullness of joy—therefore I declare that I will let you take my hand each day and lead me to the place where you share your secrets with me and pour out your love upon me. You are my home base for all my days!

DAY TWENTY-FOUR
Overwhelming Joy

And whenever the living creatures give glory, honor, and thanks to the One seated on the throne who lives forever and ever, the twenty-four elders fall down before the One seated on the throne, and they worship Him who lives forever and ever. They cast their crowns before the throne, saying: "Worthy are You, our Lord and God, to receive glory and honor and power, for You created all things; by Your will they exist and came to be."
(Revelation 4:9-11)

There are moments amid deep times of worship that suddenly we find ourselves overwhelmed by the awe and the beauty of the "One who is seated upon the throne." If we had crowns, we would surely cast them on the ground before him. Often the glory knocks our knees out from under us and we drop to the ground in worship. It is in the moments of giving glory, honor and thanks to him that we are caught up in what is happening in heaven before his throne.

I have been blessed to have had some amazing experiences with God throughout the years. A few have come at random and unexpected times, but most have come during those times where my heart was pouring out glory, honor, and thanks to my Lord. I honestly believe that as we posture our lives like the twenty-four elders before his throne, there is a supernatural connection with the worship that is happening in heaven that draws us in. My husband and I spent several years as the directors of a house of prayer. During those years, it was like being a part of the heavenly procession day after day. It brought us great joy to spend those years set apart to pray and worship day after day.

Not everyone has the opportunity to be a part of a house of prayer where they can spend day after day. Still, the one thing that I have learned is that we can posture our lives in a place of constant prayer and worship—while working, raising families, driving, cleaning house, or whatever we are doing. The Holy Spirit is always active within us, and we can develop a sensitivity to hearing him, to responding in worship to his revelation and to praying when he stirs our spirits. As we develop this sensitivity, what happens is that our lives become a living house of prayer. You can be ushered into the overwhelming joy of heaven's sounds, movements, intercession, and worship "as you go."

I greatly encourage you to practice and develop this sensitivity! No matter who you are or what you do for a living, you can become an earthly vessel that releases the heavenly atmosphere wherever you go. Of course, we take time for focused private and corporate prayer, and worship is essential, but I always say that Christians need to enjoy friendships, do something that feeds their soul, and just have fun. The sensitivity that you develop will make you ready in season and out of season.

I remember one year when I took my kids to our county fair. We were having fun riding rides, eating carnival food, and enjoying a summer evening when a woman and her children walked by me, and suddenly, I was overwhelmed with heaven coming to earth. God's love was poured into me for this woman like someone turned a hose of love on me. I was able to go to her and share with her what I was experiencing on her behalf. What was the most amazing thing was that she turned to me with tears in her eyes and said, "I am going through a horrible time and devastating divorce. Just five minutes ago, while I was watching my kids on the ride, I was so desperate that I cried out to God for the first time in my life and asked him if he was real."

Nurturing sensitivity to the Spirit of God creates a oneness with God. This allows you to become a vessel that can be moved and poured into at any place and any time. I can honestly say that I do not know if that woman at the fair was more blessed or if I was. I was overwhelmed with joy to be a part of her answer to her prayer: "Are you real God?" Yes, he is! Seeing her overwhelmed by the realization that God exists brought me more joy than I can express.

Be sure to develop a life that is fully connected to His Spirit so that you can be overwhelmed with joy as you journey through life.

Day Twenty-four Verse

> Complete my joy by being of the same mind, having the same love, being in full accord and of one mind. (Philippians 2:2)

DAY TWENTY-FOUR PRAYER

Holy Spirit, create in me a sensitivity to you that can be moved upon at any time. I willingly ask you to make my life a house of prayer where you can release your overwhelming love and joy. I ask that you would pour into me and pour through me to others. Overwhelm me again and again with the outpouring of who you are and how you love the world. I lay down my crown at your feet along with the twenty-four elders—you are worthy of all glory, honor and thanksgiving.

DAY TWENTY-FIVE
Grace is spelled J-o-y

One of the things that bring me constant joy is the grace of God. There is no mistake that God's grace is "Amazing Grace." His birth, his life, his death and his resurrection—it was all a gift of grace for us. We all need grace because we have all fallen short of his glorious standard. The witness of the law throughout the Old Testament's books, stories and characters proved that mankind could not uphold the law and needed grace.

No one knew that grace would come in the form of a man who was fully man and fully God. No one knew that he would come and do for all of mankind what we could not do for ourselves. Even the greatest men and women in the Bible fell short. David took another man's wife and then had him killed, Abraham took matters into his own hands to see promises fulfilled, and Elijah fled in fear and had a breakdown. Yet, from the beginning of time, there was a plan that included Amazing Grace.

I will forever be amazed that grace rescued me from a life that would have destroyed me. I was not looking for

God, but he was looking for me. He met me time and time again when I needed him most and drew me to him through his patient pursuit of love. He wasn't in a hurry but kept extending grace to invite me into a discovery with his love and kindness. As I look back on the journey I took as I came to know him, I am humbled and overcome with thanksgiving at his grace that made a way for someone so wretched. Almost forty years later it still brings me into a place of wonder and takes me to the point of tears. What grace—undeserved, unsought, unconditional, and completely amazing.

> …looking to Jesus, the founder and perfecter of our faith, who for the joy that was set before him endured the cross, despising the shame, and is seated at the right hand of the throne of God.
> (Hebrews 2:2)

What joys await those who have embraced this life of grace. It's like winning an eternal lottery, except this "lottery" is offered to all to stand as a winner—they only must accept their prize—Jesus. Every debt is paid in full! All our sins, our failures, our shortcomings, and our selfish choices are removed by the blood and grace of Jesus. He took them all upon himself to give us freedom and eternal life. Such amazing grace that spells out JOY for us.

Day Twenty-five Verse

For by grace you have been saved through faith, and that not of yourselves; it is the gift of God, not of works, lest anyone should boast
(Ephesians 2:8-9)

Day Twenty-five Prayer

God, I declare over my life and before all of heaven and earth that grace is the greatest reason for joy that anyone could ever have. Amazing grace has washed over me and cleansed me from all my sin and failure. It has paid my debts and canceled my punishment. I choose to surrender deeper into the unlimited pool of grace that is offered by the Father, Son, and Holy Spirit. How joyful I am for the grace by which I have been saved.

DAY TWENTY-SIX
The Joy of Being Known

> Now I know in part; then I shall know fully, even as I am fully known. (1 Corinthians 13:12)

Even as I am fully known. I am fully known and yet fully loved. That may be one of the most wonderous statements ever made. God knows you better than you know yourself—and he still loves you and loves to be in relationship with you. He loves you so much that he calls you his bride.

It wrecks me how much he loves you and me. There is great beauty within us that is joined with great need and vulnerability. Jesus meets that need with the fullness of who he is. Do you ever feel forgotten or invisible? Have you felt alone in a crowd or crowded by your loneliness? There has not been a moment in your life that you were ever actually alone, forgotten, or invisible. You are the absolute focus of the attention and affection of God. He knows every thought, every longing, every desire, every disappointment, and even every hair upon your head. Even when you do not feel intimately joined to him, he is more intimate with you than you can ever comprehend.

Galatians 4:9 says,

> But now that you know God--or rather are known by God--how is it that you are turning back to those weak and miserable forces? Do you wish to be enslaved by them all over again?

I believe that most people who have known God (and are known by him) lose their way when they forget how intimately he knows them and how very much he still loves them. Being known by God is an integral part of our identity. When we are known, it makes room to be real, vulnerable, and humble. Where do people act the most natural? At home with the people who love and know them. They can be silly, serious, sad, or spiritual. There is no need for pretenses. But sometimes, I watch believers begin to act and talk different when they begin to pray or spend time with God. He is your Father and your family—he wants you to be who you are with no pretenses or masks.

Religion often gives the message that we need to "act" spiritual. The truth is that who you are is absolutely spiritual and acceptable to God. You were created in his image, yet often we do not recognize his image within us—but he does! You are known in your room alone when no one is looking, you are known in the crowds, and he can pick out your laughter among all the noise, you are known when you feel scared or insecure and need his help and you are known when you are on your knees in worship—it is the sweetest sound he has ever heard.

On day ten, I wrote about one very painful season, and how God in his kindness "danced over me" I had felt on display because everyone at our church knew what I was going through. The vulnerability that I felt left me feeling exposed, and I wondered if there was anyone who really understood the loneliness I felt at that time. Then came the Sunday I heard the Lord say to me, "Kathi, today I am going to break the isolation that you feel. Watch as I dance around you."

About an hour into our service the Holy Spirit broke out with such a sweet and tangible presence. I was standing over the side of the stage, lost in worship; then I heard him say, "Open your eyes." I opened my eyes, and a group of people from our congregation had encircled me and were dancing around me. When I saw this, I fell to my knees, and it began a significant breakthrough in my life. I was known by God! My sorrows turned to joy, and my tears turned to laughter.

What joy it is to be known by God. You are known!

Day Twenty-six Verse

"Before I formed you in the womb, I knew you,
And before you were born, I consecrated you;
I have appointed you a prophet to the nations."
(Jeremiah 1:5)

DAY TWENTY-SIX PRAYER

I am known by God! I will not forget this amazing truth. I am known, I am loved, and I am wanted. He is not ashamed of me or disappointed in me. He is filled with great joy regarding me, he dances over me, and he grants me joy that turns my tears into laughter. I was made in his image and known before I was ever born. Abba, you are my joy, and I am yours. Being known gives me identity and purpose—it gives me freedom!

DAY TWENTY-SEVEN
Healing Joy

> The LORD your God is in your midst, a mighty one
> who will save; he will rejoice over you with gladness;
> he will quiet you by his love; he will exult over you
> with loud singing. (Zephaniah 3:17)

The day the Lord "danced around me" marked the beginning of moving into a joy I had not previously encountered. I had experienced him quieting me by his love but the rejoicing over me with gladness and the exulting over me with loud singing was a new experience for me. I had known his comfort but was becoming acquainted with his joy over me. Have you had the taste of his experiential joy over who you are and how much he loves you? If not, it is time.

Just a year and a half after coming to know the Lord, he had turned my entire life from ashes to beauty. I was in a constant state of awe as I watched his faithfulness fill every aspect of my life. I was a mere nineteen years old, and I was about to walk down the aisle of the church to be joined in marriage to my husband. As I stood waiting to walk down the aisle, I was hit by the most extraordinary joy. I was looking out on a church filled with beautiful family and friends with the man I was going to be joined with in marriage, waiting for me to walk to him. It was truly a dream-come-true and a "more than you can ask or imagine" moment.

My life had been so painful in my first eighteen years, and the next year and a half was an experience of being healed by the joy of his strength and love. His extravagant love had not only filled my heart and soul, but it had filled my days, my new relationships, and my new life. Every part of my life was being healed by joy. In those days, I would often find myself driving down the road, and I'd break into laughter at how joyful and happy I was—and how overwhelmed I was with being loved by Jesus. Oh, take us all back to that first love experience.

> "Heal me, LORD, and I will be healed; save me and I will be saved, for you are the one I praise."
> (Jeremiah 17:14)

> And the people all tried to touch him, because power was coming from him and healing them all.
> (Luke 6:19)

> "But I will restore you to health and heal your wounds," declares the LORD. (Jeremiah 30:17)

He promises to restore our health and heal our wounds. Power still comes forth from him and it heals us. You can reach out to touch him and experience his power and joy.

He will rejoice over you with gladness (joy) and exult over you with singing—and it will heal you! Even as I write this, I sense that many of you are about to embark on an experience with his joy that heals. He will rejoice over you with joy, and it will heal your heart and restore your soul. Enter that joyful expectation for this to come upon your life.

Day Twenty-seven Verse

And the disciples were filled with joy and the Holy Spirit.
(Acts 13:52)

DAY TWENTY-SEVEN PRAYER

I will be filled with joy and the Holy Spirit! I believe that the joy of the Lord is healing to my body and healing to my soul. I ask you God for the experience of having your gladness and joy exulted over me. You are the source of my joy and I believe that I, too, am the subject of your joy. I receive the expressions of your joy to be made manifest in my life. Heal me and I will be healed!

DAY TWENTY-EIGHT
The Joy of New Beginnings

I love that God gives second chances and new beginnings! We all love hearing the testimonies of someone who was at rock bottom, and God reaches in at the very moment of hopeless despair and rescues them. His stories of deliverance and freedom are not only miraculous, but they give us such hope for a world that seems to be hitting "rock bottom."

I have witnessed this in my own life, in my husband's life, and in the life of my parents. My dad got saved at one of those rock bottom moments. I honestly never thought that I would see my dad come to know the Lord, but the second chance for him came at the most unexpected moment. He was at the end of a terrible, turbulent, and hateful divorce from my mom. They had both been unfaithful to one another in every way imaginable. Affairs had been happening for years, and violent rage filled the air between them. They had separated several times prior to this, but this time, the only thing left was to go to the lawyer's office and sign the decree of divorce for this unhealthy union to be finished.

I was seventeen years old and quite frankly ready to see it end. Years of living amid their turbulent relationship and betrayals had taken their toll on our entire family. I was living with my dad, and my younger brother was living with my mom—everything was a mess, and they could not even end their marriage apart from rage and hateful words. One day, I saw my dad sitting out on our deck, and I could tell that he had been crying. My heart felt compassion for him, so I went outside to sit with him. Though I had gone to church, said the salvation prayer, and desired to walk with Jesus, I had not made a solid, life-changing commitment to him. As I sat down next to my dad, I suddenly began sharing the truth of the gospel of salvation with him. It poured out of me like someone who had walked with God for many years. As I shared with him, fresh tears poured down his face, and I saw a softness come into his eyes that I had not seen before. I invited him to come to church with me the next morning, and to my surprise, he said, "Yes."

The next day he was up and dressed in a coat and tie. The anticipation on his face was clear as he rushed us through breakfast so that we would not be late. He insisted that we sit near the front of the church, and throughout worship, he wept. The words in the sermon that day seemed as though they'd been penned specifically for my dad. When the altar call was given, my dad rushed forward without hesitation. Rather than regret for the years wasted and mistakes made, hope and joy surrounded him. He was like a man who had been dying of thirst and was given a fresh cup of water that restored his soul. My dad was transformed that day from a lost and broken man to a man who had found true love.

Circumstantially, nothing had changed. He was still in the midst of an awful and bitter divorce. His children were broken, his reputation marred, and his life was a mess. But joy had just come and taken residence in his heart, and nothing compared to this joy he was experiencing—nothing could dampen the hope and joy that had come upon him through salvation.

My dad's joy did not diminish but grew with each passing day. So much so that he began to tell everyone about Jesus. The first person he had to tell was my mom. She wanted nothing to do with my dad or "his Jesus." One day, soon after his salvation, he tricked her into coming to church with him. She had been on a business trip, and he asked if he could pick her up at the airport because their divorce papers needed to be signed. But rather than signing papers, he drove straight to the church where a service was about to begin. She was furious and refused to get out of the car, but he would not budge until she agreed to go in. In anger and defeat, she went in with him. He ushered her up the front of the church where worship had begun. She sat there angry and stone-faced, but as the sound of worship filled the place, it was like a healing balm that left her defenseless to the love of God. Soon, she too began to weep. Once again, the sermon seemed to have been "penned by God." Each word was exactly what she needed to hear, and as her defenses came down, she surrendered to salvation's invitation.

The next Sunday, my dad and mom were remarried at the same altar that they both had surrendered at just days prior. Hope and joy filled that church and all who witnessed this miracle. At their recommitment ceremony, my little brother gave his life to Jesus as well. What joy heaven must have been experiencing as this miracle of new life and new beginnings were taking place. The enemy thought he had destroyed our family, but just when all hope was lost, the joy of salvation came to save the day.

There is always hope that joy will be restored, even in the most hopeless situations. If there is any area that you are feeling hopeless—take hope! God is bigger than even the most horrendous situations. What joy he brings into wrecked lives as they encounter his love. He is able to do exceedingly more than we can ask or even imagine.

Day Twenty-eight Verse

This means that anyone who belongs to Christ has become a new person. The old life is gone; a new life has begun!
(2 Corinthians 5:17)

Day Twenty-eight Prayer

I declare today that there is always hope in Jesus! Because there is hope—there is joy! I put my life fully into the grip of hope and joy that comes from a life surrendered to God. There is nothing that God cannot do to redeem my life and the life of those that I love. No circumstance, no demon, and no power can separate me from his love and his power to save. I say to my soul today, "Take joy! There is new life and new beginnings in the hands of my Savior."

DAY TWENTY-NINE
Joyful Trust

Throughout my life, I have discovered that there is something holy about a life that embraces joyful trust. Unfortunately, more and more, the world around us is filled with hopeless people who live in depression and dread. They see the condition of this world and have become victims of the temporal rather than victors of the eternal.

I have always been a "glass half full" person who expects to see God move in impossible situations. This has been such a gift from God in my life. It is not from me but from him. Even as I write this, the world around us is in so much turmoil from the pandemic, from nations falling into the hands of evil terrorist groups, and even my own nation turning into a place that is unrecognizable from the America that I grew up loving. But, something has been rising up in me that says, "Grab hold of joyful trust and expectation and do not let go." It is a holy posture! Will I look at the giants in the land and feel tiny and defeated, or will I listen for the good report and see the fruit and bounty?

It is time to become like Joshua and Caleb—to bring a good report that builds strength through joyful hope. There were many battles to face, but as long as God's children kept their hearts devoted to him, they stood victorious. He would direct them in battles from the place of victory that was promised and assured. They could go into the place of warfare with strategies from heaven that would release power from on high. Though there were giants and multitudes of enemies, the host of heaven would accompany men and women who were surrendered to God, and they would defeat great armies.

The same is true today. We have the host of heaven's armies on our side, and we can enter every battle with joyful assurance of victory. I believe that the posture of joyful trust changes the atmosphere of earth to allow heaven to come. It is holy. Even those things that appear to be losses can be turned for good as we trust God. There are times of grief, but joy comes in the morning. Expect joy to come and find your spiritual and emotional position in the place of that expectation. We are not to live in dread, but as dread champions! The enemy fears our joy and our confident assurance in our King's triumph, because it is a mighty weapon against death, depression, and dread. It is holy ground where seeds of promise grow fruit and a bountiful harvest.

Day Twenty-nine Verse

Why must I go about mourning, oppressed
by the enemy?
Send me your light and your faithful care,
let them lead me; let them bring me to your holy
mountain, to the place where you dwell.
Then I will go to the altar of God, to God, my
joy and my delight.
I will praise you with the lyre, O God, my God.
Why, my soul, are you downcast?
Why so disturbed within me?
Put your hope in God, for I will yet praise him,
my Savior and my God.
(Psalm 43:2-5)

Day Twenty-nine Prayer

Today, I turn my face away from my enemy and away from dread. I will now turn and go to the altar of God, my joy and my strength, and I will enter a posture of joyful trust. I will put my hope in God alone, and I will praise him. It is God who sets a banqueting table for me in the presence of my enemies. I will reap a fruitful harvest even as giants cast shadows that desire to provoke me to fear. I will fear the Lord only and expect to see his salvation with great joy.

DAY THIRTY

Joy's Embrace

There is little that can bring me to a place of "joyful tears" faster than watching a video of a couple, a dad and son, mother and daughter, or old friends running into each other's arms during a time of being reunited. It makes me so excited for the day that we will be reunited in heaven with the ones we deeply loved on earth, and even more, the joyful embrace we will give and receive when we see Jesus face to face.

There are different times in my life that I have lived far away from one or more of my kids. When we are apart, the longing builds in my heart with each passing day to be with them again, to hold them again, and to embrace them once again. When the time comes where we can fly to see each other, the hours on the plane cause the excitement and joy to build. When the moment of seeing the first glimpse of them arrives, there is no holding back my "mama's" feet from running to them and wrapping them in the full embrace of my love and joy. I cannot imagine what it will be like when I see the first glimpse of Jesus! The longing and anticipation have been building for almost forty years now—what a day that will be.

Joy's embrace is the climax of every believer's life. It is the moment that they live for and die for. It is what comforts us when another believer leaves this earth before us. It is what gives us hope when darkness fills the earth. It is what carries us to face another day, and it is what we long for more than any other thing. One day, sooner than we can imagine, we will not only enter into that eternal embrace of joy, but we will be reunited with children, spouses, siblings, mothers, fathers, and friends that caused our hearts to break when we were separated from them. There will be no more separation and no more heartbreak. I truly will be an eternal, joyful embrace.

> For now we see in a mirror dimly, but then face to face; now I know in part, but then I will know fully just as I also have been fully known.
> (1 Corinthians 13:12)

He is the joy set before us, and we will embrace that joy—though it feels far off, it is so much closer than we think. We cannot wait to embrace you, our beautiful Bridegroom!

Day Thirty Verse

So when Jesus had received the sour wine, He said, "It is finished!" And bowing His head, He gave up His spirit.
(John 19:30)

DAY THIRTY PRAYER

I take joy in knowing that one day I will enter your arms and never again will we be apart. I stir up my soul with joyful anticipation at the very thought that this is my destiny and will be my reality. Today I receive all the lessons of joy that I have learned in the past thirty days. I am filled with joy because of your grace, your strength, your hope and your love. I will forever find joy in the God of my salvation!

About the Author

Kathi Pelton is an author and prophetic voice to the church. She and her husband Jeffrey walk with nations and individuals to see God's original intent fulfilled on the earth, and she has spent years helping people encounter the healing love and mercy of God. Her passion is to see the establishment of genuine family gathered in the unity expressed by Jesus's prayer in John 17.

Kathi and Jeffrey married in 1983 and together have raised four children. They currently have three grandchildren, and are filled with eager expectations of many more!

The Peltons live in the Portland, Oregon region and attend Father's House City Ministries, where they serve as part of the leadership team.